Psychology of Stock Investing

From a Nobody's Point of View

Brandon Jones

XSCaPE
PUBLISHING
www.xscapepublishing.com

Our Company

In 2019, Adrian Kennedy began publishing books for independent authors from his office in Charlotte, North Carolina. His goal was to provide authors with more options and control over the publishing process at prices anyone could afford.

Today, the family owned and operated, Xscape Publishing company still continues to honor the founder's tradition of providing high-quality products and valuable services to the community.

First published by Xscape Publishing 2021

Copyright © 2021 Brandon Jones

ISBN 978-1-7351852-7-9

Brandon Jones asserts the moral right to be identified as the author of this work.

First and foremost, I want to thank Joel for showing me that stocks aren't just for stockbrokers and rich white people.

I also want to thank my board of advisors; Madu, Adrian, Josh, Stun and X for always reviewing things for me before I put them out and for being helpful in both my personal and business life.

This book is dedicated to my friends and family who believed in me, who assisted me on my journey, and showed love. You are all appreciated.

And to my son who may one day read this. This book is for you to know I'm not telling you what to buy, but how to find your own answers if you so desire to invest in stocks. Dad loves you.

Table Of Contents

1

Introduction

Hi, **I'm** one of the most known unknowns. I embarked on a journey in 2013 that, in hindsight, took me a relatively long time to really enjoy. Over time, I've developed an unorthodox way of becoming very good at most of the things that I do. Unconventional, if you will. I'm very fond of that word.

I wanted to share some of those things with you and how I became exceptional along the journey. This book is intended to be as vivid as possible, to assist you in creating a system in your head that works for you. My wish is that every one this book touches becomes a better investor or trader in the stock market.

Without taking up too much more of your time, let's get right into it. The Psychology of Stock Investing.

2

Learning The Basics

First and foremost, fear of missing out, or FOMO, is a recipe for disaster. In any field, you shouldn't jump in just because everyone else is doing it. Understand that you need to learn the basics of investing before taking action, otherwise you'll end up not only burning through the money you don't want to lose but will end up discouraging yourself as well. Nobody likes to lose, no matter what the lessons are that you learn.

I started investing back in 2013 with a fintech app called "Acorns". I believe it was the first of its kind. Back then, you could link your card, and it would round up your purchase to the nearest dollar and invest the difference. Pretty cool if you swiped your card a lot. Eventually, it did allow you to add money manually, which was better for me, seeing as I used cash a lot more back then.

Acorns was a really good app to get started with investing because it got your mind feeling good about it. But Acorns' flaw was that it auto-invested, and so you had no control over where your money was going. Let me tell you one thing about humans – we love to have some type of control. I also wanted to know more about how they were picking the stocks to invest in, and so I had to actually search YouTube because there weren't thousands of investors monetizing education on stocks back then like you have today.

This eventually led me to the app "Stash", where you could decide what stocks you wanted to invest in. At that time, I didn't have anyone in my life who was doing this, and so for me, it wasn't about fear of missing out, it was genuine curiosity. First thing I learned was to buy stock in things or places that I frequently patronized.

In 2013 I had just been discharged from the military, I was making $10/hr working at this warehouse, and I was very down in the dumps.

Because I was battling depression, I liked to drink a lot to cope. It didn't leave much room in my budget to invest, and so I made the decision to invest money every time I wanted to buy liquor. It cut down my alcohol consumption and raised my net worth by a few dollars. Luckily, I was learning how to invest in stocks, which I previously assumed that only stockbrokers could do, was becoming more and more intriguing.

As I watched more videos and did more research, something clicked with me. Warren Buffet once said something along the lines of "the stock market is transferring money from the impatient to the patient", and I sat on that thought for a while. And I was eager to invest more, but I still didn't quite know what I was doing.

Early 2014, I was more comfortable with technical analysis and getting pretty decent with picking my stocks. Until this point in time, I was not aware that you could sell, and so I kept everything I ever bought. This was inadvertently a good tax decision, even though I had maybe $800 in my account. Investing is habit-forming.

Around mid-2014, I read this book called "The Power of Habit" by Charles Duhigg and a light bulb went off in my head. I was invested in Target at the time, and when I read this book and the anecdote about how they were so good at consumer psychology, it was what I imagine a shroom trip feels like. It was a whole new world, no Aladdin.

The moment I finished reading that book, I started to look into the actual business. The CEO, the profits, how people perceived the company. I started connecting the dots and even started options trading.

My first real brokerage account was a TD Ameritrade account, back when I had to pay $7 per trade. Do you know how hard it is to profit enough to pay them $14 per trade when you're only trading with $2,000? My risk management has been very high since the beginning.

So, in 2014 I taught myself technical analysis AND how to pick stocks based on how people perceived the company. This was only the beginning for me.

3

Getting Started

I **could sit** here and make it seem like there are a million things that you should do before investing in stocks, but it's not. Once you learn the basics, which will keep you from falling flat on your face, start investing. One of the most common misconceptions, even in 2021, is that you have to have a lot of money to start.

With Fintech (Financial Technology) apps, such as M1 Finance, Cash App, and a couple others, now you can even buy fractional shares. This means that if you only have $50 to invest, and you see 2 companies you like that cost $100 each, you can invest $25 into each one and own a quarter of a share. When the shares go up a percentage, so does your $25.

This is a good way to get started because if you're not familiar with the stock market, you're mitigating your risks. On the other hand, you're growing your account so that you can eventually buy full shares and become more invested. Think of it like riding a bike with training wheels until you're ready to take them off.

I've also used M1 since 2015, and I love it. The first pie I made had 4 companies in it, and I used $300. Companies I invested in were AT&T, Clorox, Walmart, and Amazon. You could even allocate certain percentages to the pie, so each slice of the pie adds up to 100%. It not only made investing easier but also made it fun for millennials and younger generations.

Don't talk yourself out of things, talk yourself into them. Mistakes happen, and lessons are learned. It's an important part of growth. Anyone who tells you they made no mistakes aren't to be trusted. They didn't take enough risks to be truly successful.

Here's my challenge to you. Download M1. Link your bank account and whenever you want to do some frivolous spending, put 50% of it in that account. Read some of the news articles, watch some YouTube videos on consumer psychology and watch it all flow.

For the more experienced readers, I want you to think about how you got started and do you still have those core values about investing. Why or why not? Personally, some have changed. Times have changed. Those who can't adapt won't survive.

Another excuse that I hear a lot as to why people don't get started, is that they don't know how, and quite frankly, that's a horrible excuse. We live in the Information Age where even things that shouldn't be publicized are often highlighted. There's no such thing as "I don't know how" anymore. There's simply "I'm not willing to learn" or "I'm not applying what I learned".

You'll find mountains of resources everywhere you look, and for some, that poses another threat to actually starting, analysis paralysis. Analysis paralysis is simply information overload. You take in so much information that you have no idea which direction to move in, so you don't move at all.

The trick here is to find enough information to simply get started, then do it. You do not have to know everything before starting. Investing is an ever-changing industry, and for that reason, it is impossible to learn everything. However, you can learn the basics and get started whenever. The basic don't change.

I think because it went from "only stock brokers can do this" to "oh, all I have to do is download this app", that made it easier for me to jump right in. I didn't have a thousand social media influencers trying to sell me information on the subject, so I didn't deal with analysis paralysis. It was simply "do this."

You have to think ahead. Your goal, if you're reading this book, is to understand stock investing and what it takes to be mentally competent in doing so, and if you never get started, you will never become competent. Allen Iverson skipped practice, not the games.

Oh, there was one other thing that I wanted to touch on, paper trading. This is where you set up what I call a "dummy" account and trade as practice. You're not losing or earning any money; you're polishing your skills. Someone recently told me that you could do it on TD Ameritrade, and I've seen it on Webull.

So, what's your excuse? You have the knowledge, you have the resources, you have the ability to invest with very little capital. The only thing stopping you is you. That's a hell of a realization, huh?

4

Researching

ighlight this next sentence. Second and third order consequences. Every action or change in a system creates a second order consequence and that consequence will create a third order consequence which helps to identify trends and find companies. These are a major key to finding good, solid companies to invest in. Whether you're trading or holding, second and third order consequences allow you to get into companies before they peak. I use this with 85% of my trades. The other 15% comes from friends and family.

I started writing a journal of my trades in December of 2019, citing article sources after I was made aware of this virus outbreak in Wuhan, China. Eventually, the outbreak would turn into a global pandemic. The point of my journal was mainly to keep track of my research methods and my train of thought. Thanks to my journaling, researching and understanding of second and third order effects, my 1-year returns for 2020 were 871%. That means every trading day I was up, on average, 3.44% because of my methods.

I knew that with an outbreak came the closings of restaurants, airlines, schools, and other major businesses and that it meant those stocks would drop. I purchased the dip. I knew that the economy would tank a bit, but that didn't really happen because the FED printed money like wild animals, so I lost some of those bets. You win some, you lose some.

Every trading day from March 17, 2020, when the country shut down until May 1, 2020, I asked myself this question: "What does this mean for the companies the lockdowns will impact?" You have to really think about these things and break them down. The better you get at thinking through things, the better you become as an investor as it relates to trading and investing based on fundamentals.

What's cool is that you can even reverse engineer that. I also asked myself: "What does this mean for the companies that supply affected companies with materials?" A lot of factories became backed up because of fewer workers being able to work in close proximity, which meant that deliveries would slow down, and which also meant that people would be turning to Amazon shopping and Amazon is really good at pivoting their lines of business quickly.

You see, there are chain reactions to all of this stuff. You just have to google and see if it's a private or public company that's being affected. You can do this with every single change in economics, politics, and even religion. All of this has an impact on the stock market.

Don't get me wrong, sometimes I do use some of these stock advisory apps like "Seeking Alpha" and "Atom Finance" to spark my ideas for what I should be doing my research on, and I strongly recommend them. You don't have to do everything using pen and paper. There're resources out there that can help smooth the process. However, don't rely solely on these resources. Do your own due diligence and research, please.

If I were an engineer or project manager, I would create a flowchart of sorts to show the chain reactions on my notes because I think it would look cool. On the other hand, I'm not writing this to look cool. It's really quite amazing to watch the dominoes fall but only when you're not one of the dominoes. Always remember, you can be one of the dominoes.

I want you to stop reading this book right now and find one company and spend 30 minutes researching it using second and third order consequences and buy it right now. If it's after hours, set a buy limit. Then come back and finish this book that I worked so hard on. Don't think about if it's too expensive, or if it's wrong, trust your due diligence. People who don't trust themselves, won't ever scale until they do. Know that when you buy, if you didn't sell at a loss, you're good. "Shoulda coulda woulda", says rapper Lil Wayne, "but you didn't..." he finishes with. There's no room for emotion when buying and selling You have no idea how many times I see "I wish I would have bought more $DUMB".

One thing you don't want to forget about when you're doing your research is sustainability. Some of these companies are one tragedy away from going bankrupt. I think Covid-19 made that clearer than ever. A lot of bottlenecks were exposed, meaning that even the businesses with better pipelines and supply chains were disrupted. Make sure the things you're investing in long-term aren't things that are here today and gone tomorrow.

Not unlike relationships, you jump in for the potential, and you hold on until you can't hold on any more. I like my companies like I like my women... focused on growth and looking good while doing it. I understand not all companies are going to be profitable, but I also understand that if you're not headed in that direction, then we can't be associated.

Speaking of associations, quickly... what publicly traded companies provide materials for Tesla? Quickly, figure that out before we move on, thank you. The answers aren't at the back of the book either, I swear. Do your research.

5

FUNDamentals

Have you figured it out yet? I hope so if you're still reading this. Anyway, I want to move on from the research because it's really not as hard as people make it seem. They just throw a lot of filler in there to upcharge you for the course. See, I told you I'm pretty good with consumer psychology. For that reason, I'm not very fond of marketing but that's another story for another book.

I may have failed to mention this earlier, but I'm also involved in real estate a bit. The reason why I chose to disclose this information now is because it's pertinent to the next thing I want to discuss, which is Funds.

I did, however, mention earlier that it doesn't take much to start investing in the stock market. While that may be true, I want to talk to you about a strategy I used when I did have a little more money to invest. It's a very simple tactic I've used to balance a 9 to 5, wholesaling and swing trading.

My job was an overnight one where I sometimes worked 16-hour shifts. Because it was so lax, I was able to work on wholesaling, research the stock market and even learn a little coding while on my shift. To me, it was the perfect setup for allocating funds. I took advantage beautifully, if I do say so myself.

Because I lived in the hood, my expenses weren't very high, and I was making decent money for someone living in Memphis. I was bringing home around $3,300 every 2 weeks after taxes (I didn't know then that the IRS taxed you on overtime as well). My apartment rent was $450/mo, utilities maybe $250/mo, and food maybe $200/mo. I had the rest to either invest or blow it on dating. I did both.

Fast forward, I'm consistently bringing home $15K/mo from wholesaling, and at the time, I was picking up checks in my personal name and cashing them at their banks, so I wasn't really paying taxes on that money. Side note: 10 out of 10 do not recommend. Meanwhile, I'm still making $6,500/mo from my 9 to 5 and started investing $3 - $4K a month in the stock market. This is similar to building a pie in M1, except with expenses/investments. Allocation, is very important when you're starting out.

Allocation takes discipline, self-awareness, and dedication. You have to know why you're doing it, how to do it, and make mental models of how you want that to look. Take all things into consideration and save for rainy days. Practice it religiously. You should transfer this practice over to your personal life and how you manage your finances and your overall energy.

There are different subgroups of the stock market that let you invest based on your risk level. There are stocks, bonds, mutual funds, ETFs, and indexes. These vary in volatility and historic growth rate, so it's nice to have a healthy balance based on your risk tolerance.

Personally, I've always been willing to bet the house on myself. I made a mental model of how I would allocate funds to do everything I wanted. My 9 to 5 money went into my expenses and the bank, my wholesale money went into swing trading and taxes, my swing trade money went into buying rentals, my rental income went into the bank as well.

I started doing this in 2016. It was an easy way for me to keep track of where my money was coming from and going. If you have multiple streams of income, learn to allocate to maximize your efficiency. It becomes automatic and you can spend more time focusing on other things.

So, once you're investing, you need to create a mental model to allocate your funds, it actually makes it pretty entertaining. You should always know what you're investing in and you should always enjoy it.

Another important thing I learned about when investing is that "Dollar Cost Averaging" really is your best friend. DCA is beneficial for long-term investing because it allows you to get your cost basis down.

Let's say you buy 10 shares of $BREI for $10 per share. You have $100 worth of $BREI.

As you know, prices do drop. Let's say $BREI drops to $9 a share, so now you have $90 worth of the company. If you trust this company long-term, this is where you buy 10 more shares at $9, so you now have 20 shares at an average price per share of $9.50. So, when it goes back up to $10, you now have 20 shares at $9.50, and you saved 50 cents per share.

Again, this is if you trust the company. Also, this is way better than "buying the dip" because if you saw the way people tried to do that with Tesla, you'd be amazed. Some companies just don't dip when you want them to. So, buy now and buy more if it does dip.

Now that we've covered how to buy and mitigate losses, let's go over one of my favorite programs, and I think the kids can get behind this. It's called the DRIP program, short for Dividend ReInvestment Program. Make sure you have that DRIP. No need to pull out of long-term investments.

Some companies offer dividends, meaning they pay you a certain percentage of the share price for however many shares you own. With DRIP, that money can go right back into the market without you ever thinking about it. I'm not sure if all brokerages have it, but I know for sure that TD Ameritrade does.

I don't focus on which companies pay out the most dividends because I like my companies to put their money back in the company, and that's usually the difference between companies that do pay dividends and those that don't.

6

Strategy

Whether you're building a long-term portfolio, swing trading, day trading, or trading options, you need a strategy. Without one, you'll probably lose more money than you'll make. Strategies help market research become easier, helps you stay disciplined, and helps you build mental models for other areas of your life.

When I first started investing, I used the good ol' fundamental "buy what you frequently use/buy" method, and it worked. Then as I became more comfortable with my market research, I started looking into other companies that I'd see when I was out in public. What made me decide to buy or not is a story for another day.

As I began swing trading, I had to develop more strategies. First was funding. I took some of my money from real estate and stuck it into companies that I researched and liked. At this point, trends in the economy and how the market moved accordingly had sparked my interest. All that was needed was for me to stick to the plan, and I could make money even quicker than wholesaling. That's exactly what happened.

This brought on a system for connecting all my major streams of income. My 9-5 was for bills, living, play stuff. I would then take my wholesale money, put away money for taxes and stick another 50% of each deal into a company. I would then take the profits every 4-6 weeks and buy a property with the swing trade profits and a wholesale deal. Rinse and repeat.

This kept me from taking out loans for properties or renovations. It worked wonders for me. I eventually tweaked the system to include business acquisitions and some other stuff, but that was the foundation. Whatever you do, build systems to make it easier on you.

You may be wondering why I decided that was a good idea. I thought it would be easier for me to move my money in a cycle than it would be to take care of everything separately.

As far as my long-term portfolio was concerned, my system was simple. I purchased companies that paid dividends, used the dividends to purchase other shares of companies that I figured would be around and progressive. I only checked my long-term portfolio once a quarter. We have this saying that goes "buy it and take a nap". That means invest in the company then forget it's there.

I find it very entertaining to be aggressive with investing in your earlier years. Having to learn to allocate, entry and exit points, losing and making money, just learning the market in general. Especially in this bull run where it seems you can't lose for long.

7

Scaling

Have you ever read a book that had a chapter with only three sentences? Here's one. The only way to scale investing is to buy more.

8

Long-Term Investing

There are so many ways to make money in the stock market. You have options, day trading, swing trading, and my favorite, long-term investing. Long-term, and I mean until retirement age, is a savings plan on steroids. Well, if done right.

Long-term investing requires very little maintenance because depending on your age, you're probably not going to be 65 before you see some serious gains. This does depend on what you're investing in, so don't just go throwing darts at a board.

I set up my Roth IRA in 2018 when I started my first business and just let it sit. Most companies will stick your money into a mutual fund and call it a day. I stuck mine in companies like Walmart, Boeing, Amazon, etc. These are companies I believe will continue to grow faster than the S&P 500 until I'm 65.

That's basically what you're looking for with long-term investing. Companies that can withstand the test of time. I only check my long-term portfolios once a quarter or when I want to add something. The only other time I check it is when I get news of something horrible going on with the economy or one of the companies you invest in specifically. And don't look at your portfolio every day unless you're journaling because it will drive you absolutely insane.

There're also tax advantages to holding 401Ks, Roth, and Roth IRAs. Long-term investing is designed to keep you well off.

Question, how long can you wait to see a 1000% return? Do you REALLY need that right now? Allocate some money to have when you're done working and forget how to swing trade or trade options.

9

Swing Trading

What is swing trading? Swing trading is buying shares of companies and holding for a relatively short period of time. This is good for building capital but should be done only after you've started your long-term investing.

Swing trading takes discipline. You'll have to know when to buy and when to sell. You have to be ok with buying and selling too early. "Diamond hands" is a term used by traders that describes when a stock is down and a trader is holding because they have faith in the company making them a profit.

It helps to know why you're buying it. A general rule of thumb is to "buy the rumor and sell the news". The psychology behind that is most stocks will rise between the time they're rumored to do something and the time the news actually confirms, where it will then slow down on the growth.

Speaking of growth, what I found to be more efficient with swing trading and growing my account was finding one or two emerging sectors and swinging the companies in those sectors. It makes the research a lot easier when you know what the company is supposed to be doing.

One thing I see with a lot of swing traders is "I sold too early". Pigs get slaughtered. Treat a swing like an ex-girlfriend, once you're done, don't go checking on how she's doing. That's not good for your mental health. The stock has moved on, and so should you.

Time in a trade isn't really a factor, but I swing for around 4-6 weeks or until I hit my 30% goal if it happens before then. I don't want to tie up my money too long, and I don't need to hit a home run every time. I also don't want to lose paper gains waiting on bigger gains when there's other plays to be made.

Speaking of losing gains, set stop losses. Some things to take into consideration when setting stop losses is how much you're willing to lose not only financially but mentally. You may be ok with losing $5,000 in a single trade financially, but if it's going to make you desperate to win it back, then your stop loss should be way before that. Desperation is the quickest way to lose money in the stock market.

"The stock market is a way of transferring money from the impatient to the patient", or whatever Warren Buffet said. It is incredibly true. Take your time, learn the fundamentals and prosper.

Losses are a part of the game. You win some, you lose some, but you live to invest another day. Losses are actually great in the sense that you can learn what makes the market move in what direction. I'd like to take the time to note that a trading journal is important for the lessons you learn to be useful information.

Losses are horrible in the sense that if you sell, you lose that money, albeit temporarily. You still have a chance to make it back. Cutting your losses is important because sometimes a company is just not good on paper for a while *cough* $ATT *cough* and you can make up for that loss elsewhere.

Knowing when to take your loss is subjective in amount but imperative in principle. You don't want to wake up down 50% because you got in a bad trade and wanted to have "diamond hands". Every brokerage allows you to set stop losses so you won't lose money in your sleep. Can't beat that.

10

Ending

I **started investing in 2013,** so this book is in no way meant to be taken as financial advice. This came about from frequently asked questions from the internet and a desire to entertain. I have personally made some good investments in the stock market. I bought a lot of shares of this tech company a year or two ago, and I am up 1,306% as of today.

I've also gone to sleep and forgot about a trade I was up 30% on and woke up to it being down 50%. No, I did not exercise diamond hands, I sold for a loss. My taxes won't be mad at all. Short term capital gains are something else.

Before I go, I want to note that during the time I started and finished this book, there was a war waged against hedge funds where companies like $AMC and $GME were being shorted by hedge funds because of the coronavirus and some people decided to band together and do what's called a short squeeze. What they did was run the price up so the hedge funds would lose money.

One company during this time was down $13 billion at one point. In unprecedented moves, several brokerages stopped trading in certain stocks and put restrictions on a lot more. This even included the options on the stocks that had trading limitations. The story is still developing as of this moment, but I'm just glad I have the pleasure of living in one of the most entertaining times in Wall Street history.

Read this book, take some notes, buy you some stock in companies you won't have to worry about for years to come (unless you're reading this at 64) and enjoy life.

CPSIA information can be obtained
at www.ICGtesting.com
Printed in the USA
JSHW021037090521
14545JS00004B/5